N OF MAN

BREAD OF LIF

KING OF KINGS

LAMB OF GOD

REDEEMER

IMMANUEL

SAVIOR

LORD

MESSIAH

TEACHER

SON OF GOD

PRINCE OF PEACE

CHRIST

GHT OF THE WORLD

GOOD SHEPHERD

SON OF MAN

BREAD OF LIFE

KING OF KINGS

LAMB OF GOD

REDEEMER

IMMANUEL

SAVIOR

LORD

TEACHER

MESSIAH

SON OF GOD

PRINCE OF PEACE

CHRIST

LIGHT OF THE WORLD

GOOD SHEPHERD

HIS NAME IS

JESUS

HIS NAME IS JESUS
PERSONAL REFLECTIONS AND SCRIPTURE ABOUT THE BEAUTIFUL NAMES OF CHRIST
INTRODUCTION BY PHILIP YANCEY

His Name Is Jesus
Copyright 1998 by ZondervanPublishingHouse

ZondervanPublishingHouse
Grand Rapids, Michigan
A Division of *HarperCollins*Publishers

ISBN 0310973635

Requests for information should be addressed to:

ZondervanPublishingHouse
Mail Drop B20
Grand Rapids, Michigan 49530
http://www.zondervan.com

Senior Editor: Gwen Ellis
Compiled by Jean E. Syswerda
Designed by Pam Moore of Steve Diggs and Friends
Interior layout by Jody A. DeNeef

Printed in China

99 00 01 02 03/HK/9 8 7 6 5 4 3 2

Contents

A WORD ABOUT JESUS FROM PHILIP YANCEY

Jesus embodies the promise of a god
who will go to any length to win us back.
not the least of jesus' accomplishments
is that he made us somehow lovable to god.

PHILIP YANCEY

Does any human emotion run as deep as hope? Fairy tales, for example, pass down from generation to generation a belief in the impossibly happy ending, an irrepressible sense that in the end the forces of evil will lose the struggle and the brave and good will some-how triumph.

For the Jews in Palestine 2000 years ago, all hope seemed like a fairy tale. No prophet had spoken to them in 400 years. They waited and wondered. And then something momentous happened. The birth of a baby was announced—a birth unlike any that had come before. The birth of One whose name would be . . . Jesus.

Two thousand years after that birth, I spent a long night of sitting in an uncomfortable Naugahyde chair in O'Hare Airport, waiting impatiently for a flight that was delayed for five hours. I happened to be sitting next to a wise woman who was traveling to the same conference as I. The long delay and the late hour combined to create a melancholy mood, and in five hours we had time to share all the dysfunctions of childhood, our disappointments with the church, our questions of faith.

My companion listened to me for a very long time, and then out of nowhere she asked a question that has always stayed with me. "Philip, do you ever just let God love you?" she said.

I realized with a start that she had brought to light a gaping hole in my spiritual life. For all my absorption in the Christian faith, I had missed the most important message of all. The story of Jesus is the story of a celebration, a story of love. It involves pain and disappointment, yes, for God as well as for us. But Jesus embodies the promise of a God who will go to any length to win us back. Not the least of Jesus' accomplishments is that he made us somehow lovable to God.

For God so loved the world that he gave his one and only Son, that whoever believes in him shall not perish but have eternal life. For God did not send his Son into the world to condemn the world, but to save the world through him.

JOHN 3:16, 17

SIMON PETER

ANSWERED,

"YOU ARE THE

CHRIST,

THE SON OF THE

LIVING GOD."

MATTHEW 16:16

JESUS

CHRIST

I have an unquenchable desire to slow down and find my life going deeper in my walk with Christ. I want to meet him in the depths of my soul, away from the stress and press of everything on top. A relationship with Christ is the key to fulfilling our deepest longings. All of life is about filling the void that sin and separation from him have created within. Filling the emptiness with piles of things, earthly friendships, satisfying experiences, and sensual encounters ultimately proves to achieve less than what we had hoped for. Christ is the only one who fits.

JOSEPH M. STOWELL

I once read in a Bible commentary that the word "Christian" means "Little Christs." What an honor to share Christ's name! We can be bold to call ourselves Christians and bear the stamp of his character and reputation. When people find out that you are a Christian, they should already have an idea of who you are and what you are like simply because you bear such a precious name.

JONI EARECKSON TADA

Christ is the first title given to our Lord in the New Testament. Matthew 1 contains a host of names, covering three periods of fourteen generations each, but one Name stands out like a radiant star to lighten all the others; one Person to whom all must render allegiance — Jesus (Savior) Christ (the Anointed One). At his feet every knee shall bow in heaven and on earth.

**T.C. HORTON &
CHARLES E. HURLBURT**

Those who walk with Christ by faith know the meaning of wonder in their daily lives. Ordinary people experience extraordinary things because of the wonder of Christ. These wonders may not be obvious to those outside the family of God, but they're clearly visible to those inside the family. His wonders are seen in so-called little things, such as a flower, or bird, or a baby's smile. And they're seen in big things as well, such as the courage to say "No" or the strength to keep going when the road is difficult. Little things become big things when they're touched by the wonder of Christ.

WARREN W. WIERSBE

"I AM THE GOOD SHEPHERD. THE GOOD SHEPHERD LAYS DOWN HIS LIFE FOR THE SHEEP."

JOHN 10:11

JESUS

GOOD SHEPHERD

To say, "The Lord is my shepherd," must carry with it in our understanding not merely grateful praise for the infinite grace and tenderness of the Great Shepherd who leads us by still waters and in green pastures, but confession of our own helplessness and need of a Shepherd's care. And a remembrance also of our lost, undone condition.

**T. C. HORTON &
CHARLES E. HURLBURT**

The King of love my Shepherd is,
Whose goodness faileth never,
I nothing lack if I am His
And He is mine forever.

Perverse and foolish oft I strayed,
But yet in love He sought me,
And on His shoulder gently laid,
And home, rejoicing, brought me.

And so through all the length of days
Thy goodness faileth never;
Good Shepherd, may I sing Thy praise
Within Thy house forever.

SIR HENRY WILLIAMS BAKER

The Lord's my Shepherd, I'll not
   want.
He makes me down to lie
In pastures green; He leadeth me
The quiet waters by.

My soul He doth restore again;
And me to walk doth make
Within the paths of righteousness,
Even for His own Name's sake.

Yea, though I walk in death's dark
   vale,
Yet will I fear no ill;
For Thou art with me; and Thy rod
And staff my comfort still.

My table Thou hast furnished
In presence of my foes;
My head Thou dost with oil anoint,
And my cup overflows.

Goodness and mercy all my life
Shall surely follow me;
And in God's house forevermore
My dwelling place shall be.

FROM THE
SCOTTISH PSALTER

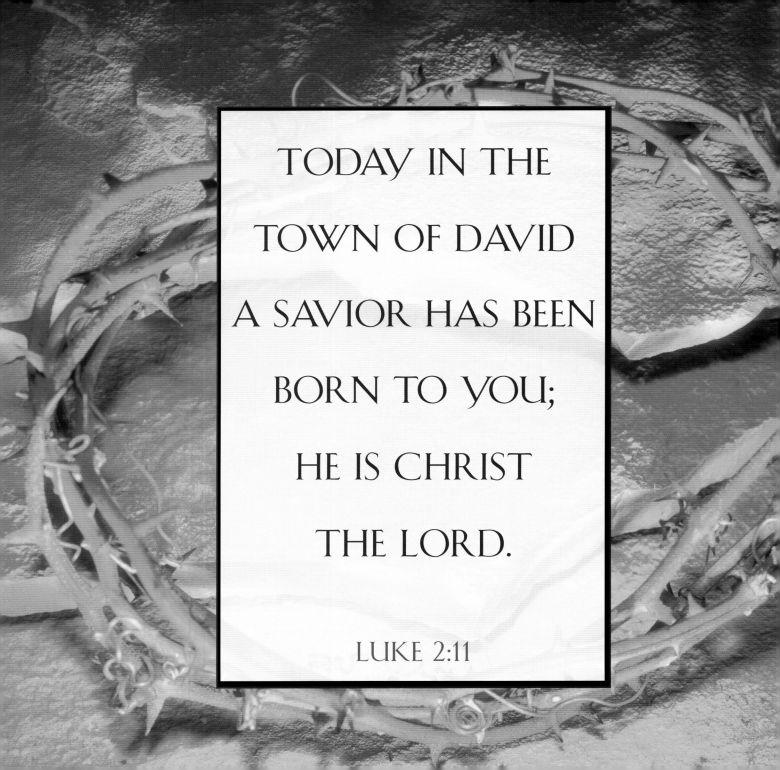

TODAY IN THE
TOWN OF DAVID
A SAVIOR HAS BEEN
BORN TO YOU;
HE IS CHRIST
THE LORD.

LUKE 2:11

JESUS

SAVIOR

There are a thousand different ways to respond to the news that a Savior has been born to deliver people from their sins. But the fact remains that until a child was born, this world was cloaked in utter darkness, abandoned, hopeless, and lost. But for unto us, a child is born, a Son is given! There is only one response: Worship and joyous praise!

JONI EARECKSON TADA

You have trusted Christ as your dying Savior; now trust Him as your living Savior. Just as much as He came to deliver you from future punishment, did He also come to deliver you from present bondage. Just as truly as He came to bear your stripes for you, has He come to live your life for you. You could as easily have got yourself rid of your own sins, as you could now accomplish for yourself practical righteousness. Christ, and Christ only, must do both for you.

HANNAH WHITALL SMITH

*Sun of my soul, Thou Savior
   dear,*
It is not night if Thou be near;
O may no earthborn cloud arise
*To hide Thee from Thy servant's
   eyes.*

Abide with me from morn till eve,
For without Thee I cannot live;
Abide with me when night is nigh,
For without Thee I dare not die.

JOHN KEBLE

Man of Sorrows! what a name
For the Son of God, Who came
Ruined sinners to reclaim.
Hallelujah! What a Savior!

Bearing shame and scoffing rude,
In my place condemned He stood;
Sealed my pardon with His blood.
Hallelujah! What a Savior!

Lifted up was He to die;
"It is finished!" was His cry;
Now in heaven exalted high.
Hallelujah! What a Savior!

When He comes, our glorious King,
All His ransomed home to bring,
Then anew His song we'll sing;
Hallelujah! What a Savior!

PHILIP PAUL BLISS

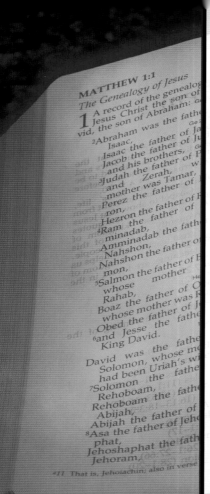

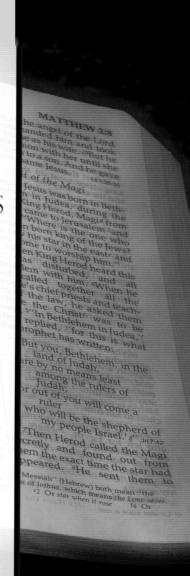

WHEN THE CENTURION
AND THOSE WITH HIM
WHO WERE GUARDING JESUS
SAW THE EARTHQUAKE AND
ALL THAT HAD HAPPENED,
THEY WERE TERRIFIED,
AND EXCLAIMED, "SURELY
HE WAS THE SON OF GOD!"

MATTHEW 27:54

JESUS

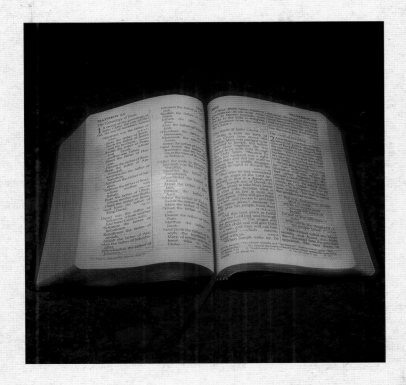

SON *of* GOD

Strong Son of God, immortal love,
Whom we, that have not seen Thy face,
By faith, and faith alone, embrace,
Believing where we cannot prove.

Thou seemest human and divine,
The highest, holiest manhood, Thou.
Our wills are ours, we know not how;
Our wills are ours, to make them Thine.

ALFRED, LORD TENNYSON

The Son of God dropped to the dirt in an olive grove—Gethsemane—and vomited in his soul at the prospect before him. Eleven men who would later change world history—some accustomed to working all night on their fishing boats—could not keep awake for the scene. Yet sixty feet away their eternal destinies were being fought over. Except for the heaving of those shoulders that bore the weight of the world, nothing could be seen in that shadowy spot where the Son of God groaned. But the bleachers of heaven filled to capacity that night—and hell strained its neck to see how the spectacle in that lonely acre would end. The Father gazed down and gave his sober nod. The Son stared back, and bowed his acceptance.

JONI EARECKSON TADA
STEVE ESTES

Your voice alone, O Lord, can speak
    to me of grace;
Your power alone, O Son of God, can all
    my sin erase.
No other work but Thine, no other blood
    will do;
No strength but that which is divine can
    bear me safely through.

I praise the Christ of God; I rest on love
    divine;
And with unfaltering lip and heart I call
    this Savior mine.
My Lord has saved my life and freely
    pardon gives;
I love because He first loved me, I live
    because He lives.

HORATIUS BONAR

In Mark 5 we are confronted with a testimony from an unclean spirit— "Son of the Most High God," he calls Jesus. What unseen powers compelled this significant title? Was it brought about by being face to face with Jesus himself? Judas betrayed him, but this poor, demon-possessed man worshiped him. In these strange days many . . . refuse to honor him as the Son, but only as a Son of God. But we lift our hearts to him and say, "Son of the Most High God . . ."

**T.C. HORTON &
CHARLES E. HURLBURT**

WHEN JESUS SPOKE AGAIN
TO THE PEOPLE, HE SAID,
"I AM THE LIGHT OF THE
WORLD. WHOEVER FOL-
LOWS ME WILL NEVER
WALK IN DARKNESS,
BUT WILL HAVE
THE LIGHT OF LIFE."

JOHN 8:12

JESUS

LIGHT *of the* WORLD

Take away the sun from our system, and all would be darkness and death. So the human race without a Savior is a ruin, and the soul, without a spiritual sun to enlighten it, a desolation. But Jesus says, "I am the light of the world. Whoever follows me will never walk in darkness, but will have the light of life" (John 8:12).

JAMES LANGE

Lord Jesus, light of the world, Your light shows me the truth about myself and Your strength gives me courage to change those things that need to be changed. Your light also reveals the things You want to affirm. In Your presence, the miracle happens again. You bring out of hiding the person You want to liberate and affirm. It's wonderful to know that You know the most profound longing of my heart: to love and serve You, to be loyal and faithful to You, and to love others as You have loved me.

LLOYD JOHN OGILVIE

The whole world was lost
In the darkness of sin,
The light of the world is Jesus!
Like sunshine at noonday,
His glory shone in.
The light of the world is Jesus!

No darkness have we
Who in Jesus abide;
The light of the world is Jesus!
We walk in the light
When we follow our guide!
The light of the world is Jesus!

Come to the light, 'tis shining for thee;
Sweetly the light has dawned upon me.
Once I was blind, but now I can see:
The light of the world is Jesus!

PHILIP PAUL BLISS

Don't be fearful about the journey ahead; don't worry about where you are going or how you are going to get there. If you believe in the First Person of the Trinity, God the Father, also believe in the Second Person of the Trinity, the One who came as the Light of the World, not only to die for people, but to light the way . . . This One, Jesus Christ, is Himself the Light and will guide your footsteps along the way.

EDITH SCHAEFFER

"THE VIRGIN WILL BE WITH

CHILD AND WILL GIVE

BIRTH TO A SON, AND

THEY WILL CALL HIM

IMMANUEL" — WHICH

MEANS, "GOD WITH US."

MATTHEW 1:23

JESUS

IMMANUEL

Christ, by highest heav'n
   adored; Christ the everlasting
   Lord;
Late in time, behold Him come,
   offspring of a virgin's womb.
Veiled in flesh the Godhead see;
   hail th'incarnate Deity,
Pleased with us in flesh to dwell,
   Jesus our Immanuel.

CHARLES WESLEY

There is another truth that comes from the name "Immanuel." Not only is Jesus Christ eternal, God, but he is God with us. He isn't a God who is far away, distant, and unconcerned; he's with us where we are, sharing the experiences of our lives. When Jesus Christ was born of the Virgin Mary and came in this world as a little baby, he identified with all aspects of humanity. He is the God-man, he is God, and he is God with us.

WARREN W. WIERSBE

Immanuel (God with us)! What a wonderful God and Savior he is and he is with us as he promised. Let us sense his presence and make him real. Walk, talk, live with and love him more and more as the days go by.

**T. C. HORTON &
CHARLES E. HURLBURT**

Joseph, son of David," the angel said, "you should not fear to take Mary home as your wife. . . . She will bear a son, and when she does you must call his name Jesus, since he will save his people from their sins.

"God is fulfilling prophecies, Joseph!

His name shall be called Immanuel.

*"Immanuel," the angel said.
"Immanuel, God with us."*

WALTER WANGERIN

THE NEXT DAY JOHN

SAW JESUS COMING

TOWARD HIM AND SAID,

"LOOK, THE LAMB OF

GOD, WHO TAKES AWAY

THE SIN OF THE WORLD!"

JOHN 1:29

JESUS

LAMB *of* GOD

How shall we say in a few words that which springs up in our hearts and would break forth from our lips? "The Lamb of God who bears away our sin." . . . He bore the sins of those who received him while here on the earth and he bore them away when he paid the penalty on the cross and shed his atoning blood. God's Lamb! No one else could be God's Lamb. He was the voluntary offering. What can we do? Believe it, accept it, take our place with him.

**T. C. HORTON &
CHARLES E. HURLBURT**

Just as I am, without one plea,
But that Thy blood was shed for me,
And that Thou bidst me come to Thee,
O Lamb of God, I come, I come.

Just as I am, poor, wretched, blind;
Sight, riches, healing of the mind,
Yea, all I need in Thee to find,
O Lamb of God, I come, I come.

Just as I am, Thy love unknown
Hath broken every barrier down;
Now, to be Thine, yea, Thine alone,
O Lamb of God, I come, I come.

CHARLOTTE ELLIOTT

The most significant event of the centuries took place in . . . a stable. I wonder what Mary thought? Haven't you wondered what went through her mind as she saw that little one? The most significant thing that happened didn't happen in Caesar's court or in Quirinius's palace or among the plans of the Jewish zealots to overthrow Rome. The most significant thing happened in a manger. Yes, Mary had a little Lamb that night. And her precious little Lamb was destined for sacrifice. There was a tiny Lamb in Bethlehem who was destined for Golgotha's altar.

CHARLES R. SWINDOLL

O Lord Jesus, Lamb of God,
Bearing such a heavy load;
Pain and suffering was Your fate—
Anguish, ridicule and hate.

Tree of anguish, bear my sin;
Heart of Jesus, let me in.
O Lord, may Your wounds make
*   whole*
Body, spirit and my soul.

ROBERT CULLINAN

THEN JESUS DECLARED,

"I AM THE BREAD OF LIFE.

HE WHO COMES

TO ME WILL NEVER

GO HUNGRY, AND HE

WHO BELIEVES IN ME

WILL NEVER BE THIRSTY."

JOHN 6:35

JESUS

BREAD *of* LIFE

When we come to the Bread of Life, Jesus himself, we continue to be fed by "every word that comes from the mouth of God" (Matthew 4:4), in his written Word. It has been supernaturally kneaded. The ingredients needed for strength and help have been mixed in. It has been prepared. Long ago? Yes, but fresh every day.

EDITH SCHAEFFER

Answering humanity's cry . . . Jesus says, "I am the bread of life," the life-eternal-giving Bread. This reply settles the question forever. He is the true Bread, the Bread of God, and the Bread of life. How is this Bread to be dispensed? It must be made known to an ignorant world. The terms upon which it is to be received must be made clear and definite. "Come to me," says Jesus, "and you shall never hunger."

T. C. HORTON & CHARLES E. HURLBURT

Lord Christ, the Bread of Life, what physical bread is for the body, you are for my hungry heart. You alone can save, satisfy, and strengthen my inner being. My hunger to know you better is a sure evidence that I belong to you. My heartaches are an indication of how much I need you. Bread of life, you satisfy my deepest needs for love, self-esteem, significance, affirmation, a reason for living, involvement in a calling that counts, an assurance that there is meaning in daily living. You give me security no one else can provide.

LLOYD JOHN OGILVIE

Jesus, Thou Joy of loving hearts,
Thou Fount of life, Thou Light of men,
From the best bliss that earth imparts,
We turn unfilled to Thee again.

Thy truth unchanged hath ever stood;
Thou savest those that on Thee call;
To them that seek Thee Thou art good,
To them that find Thee all in all.

We taste Thee, O Thou living Bread,
And long to feast upon Thee still;
We drink of Thee, the Fountainhead,
And thirst our souls from Thee to fill.

BERNARD OF CLAIRVAUX

SIMON PETER
ANSWERED HIM,
"LORD, TO WHOM
SHALL WE GO?
YOU HAVE THE WORDS
OF ETERNAL LIFE.
WE BELIEVE AND
KNOW THAT YOU
ARE THE HOLY
ONE OF GOD."

JOHN 6:68 – 69

JESUS

LORD

If Jesus is Lord then the only right response to him is surrender and obedience. He is Savior and he is Lord. We cannot separate his demands from his love. We cannot dissect Jesus and relate only to the parts that we like or need. Christ died so that we could be forgiven for managing our own lives. It would be impossible to thank Christ for dying and yet to continue running our own lives.

REBECCA PIPPERT

There is no room in Scripture for a one-sided view of our Lord. Jesus always oversteps the comfort zones of people. He hits the light switch in stuffy rooms of darkness and evil. He barges into our lives, tearing aside the curtains we've tried to pull over secret sins. He heaves his shoulder against the doors we've locked to protect private habits from his scrutiny. Our Lord always "talks out of turn," such as around banquet tables with prominent guests of honor. Always, always he urges some inconvenient, untimely change in people's lives.

JONI EARECKSON TADA

Lord of all being, throned afar,
Thy glory flames from sun and star;
Center and soul of every sphere,
Yet to each loving heart how near!

Lord of all life, below, above,
Whose light is truth, Whose warmth is
love,
Before Thy ever blazing throne
We ask no luster of our own.

Grant us Thy truth to make us free,
And kindling hearts that burn for Thee,
Till all Thy living altars claim
One holy light, one heavenly flame.

OLIVER WENDELL HOLMES

Lord, you have all authority in heaven and on earth. I submit my life to your authority. Fill my mind with clear convictions that you are in charge of my life and those about whom I am concerned. I surrender myself and them to you. There is nothing that can happen that you can't use to deepen my relationship with you. So when success comes, help me to be amazed at the way it will develop an attitude of gratitude. When difficulties arise, help me immediately turn to you and receive from you an attitude of fortitude.

LLOYD JOHN OGILVIE

AND HE WILL BE
CALLED WONDERFUL
COUNSELOR,
MIGHTY GOD,
EVERLASTING FATHER,
PRINCE OF PEACE.

ISAIAH 9:6

JESUS

PRINCE *of* PEACE

Provider of peace, give me the peace of a cleansed and committed heart, a free and forgiving heart, a caring and compassionate heart. May Your deep peace flow into me, calming my impatience and flowing from me to others. I ask this in the name of the Prince of Peace, who whispers in my soul, "Peace I leave with you."

LLOYD JOHN OGILVIE

When you think of Jesus Christ as "Prince of Peace," you immediately think of his character. Jesus was a man of peace. You see this as you watch him in the different circumstances of life. He was able to fall asleep in the ship in the midst of a storm so threatening that even his fishermen disciples were terrified. He looked at over five thousand hungry people and he knew what he would do. Our Lord's peace didn't come from the absence of trouble. It came from the depths of his soul where he fellowshiped with the Father. Peace and character go together. What we do depends a great deal on what we are. The secret of our Lord's peace was his relationship to his Father. He loved the Father, and therefore he trusted the Father. This gave him peace.

WARREN W. WIERSBE

Jesus, Lord, we look to Thee;
Let us in Thy name agree;
Show Thyself the Prince of Peace,
Bid our strife forever cease.

Make us of one heart and mind,
Gentle, courteous, and kind,
Lowly, meek, in thought and word,
Altogether like our Lord.

Let us for each other care,
Each the other's burdens bear;
To Thy church the pattern give,
Show how true believers live.

Free from anger and from pride;
Let us thus in God abide;
All the depths of love express,
All the heights of holiness.

CHARLES WESLEY

What a joy it is to know that He is what we long for most of all in this sinful, wicked, restless world—The Prince of Peace. He came to bring peace, and when He went away He said to his disciples, "Peace I leave with you; my peace I give unto you." Could there be any gift of greater value? Oh, that all might come to know Him and his peace-giving power.

**T.C. HORTON &
CHARLES E. HURLBURT**

THE FIRST THING

ANDREW DID WAS TO

FIND HIS BROTHER

SIMON AND TELL HIM,

"WE HAVE FOUND

THE MESSIAH."

JOHN 1:41

JESUS

MESSIAH

Advent recalls Israel's centuries of waiting for the Messiah. The Scripture reminds us that we, too, are waiting for God to move in our lives and in our world. Then Advent quietly insists that there is something worth waiting for. It tells us that our hope is not hollow, that as surely as God came to those people in the stable in Bethlehem, so God will come to us.

BARBARA P. FERGUSON

Jesus well understood the explosive power of the word Messiah. Although Jesus did not use the title himself, he accepted it when others called him Messiah, and the Gospels show a gradual dawning on his disciples that their teacher was none other than the long-awaited King.

PHILIP YANCEY

What a dynamic confrontation! This Man who had asked her for a simple cup of water was now standing there, claiming to be the true Messiah, holding forth living water and promising to forgive her sin and transform her. Although the text does not specifically tell us that the Samaritan woman became a believer, it seems obvious that she did. The hour of salvation had come for her. She would willingly become a true worshiper. She would drink of the Water of Life. The irresistible grace of the Messiah had penetrated her heart.

JOHN F. MACARTHUR JR.

Angels from the realm of glory,
Wing your flight over all the earth;
Ye who sang creation's story
Now proclaim Messiah's birth.

Come and worship, come and worship
Worship Christ, the newborn King.

Though an infant now we view Him,
He shall fill His Father's throne,
Gather all the nations to Him;
Every knee shall then bow down:

All creation, join in praising
God, the Father, Spirit, Son,
Evermore your voices raising
To the eternal Three in One.

JAMES MONTGOMERY

"I KNOW THAT MY

REDEEMER LIVES,

AND THAT IN THE

END HE WILL STAND

UPON THE EARTH."

JOB 19:25

JESUS

REDEEMER

There is only one relationship that matters, and that is your personal relationship to a personal Redeemer and Lord. Let everything else go, but maintain that at all costs, and God will fulfill His purpose through your life. One individual life may be of priceless value to God's purposes, and yours may be that life.

OSWALD CHAMBERS

Blessed Redeemer . . . I worship You for Your faithfulness, lovingkindness, judgment, and mercy. The offering I bring to my worship is myself. Nothing in my hands I bring; simply to Your grace I cling. The blessedness of belonging to You is the beauty of holiness I have to offer in my worship. All that I have and am belongs to You. The life You have given me is Yours, the blessings You've given me are because of Your goodness, and my triumph in the future is assured only as I trust in You alone.

LLOYD JOHN OGILVIE

Blessed Redeemer, full of compassion,
Great is Thy mercy, boundless and free;
Now in my weakness, seeking Thy favor,
Lord, I am coming closer to Thee.

Blessed Redeemer, wonderful Savior,
Fountain of wisdom, Ancient of Days,
Hope of the faithful, Light of all ages,
Jesus my Savior, Thee will I praise.

Blessed Redeemer, gracious and tender,
Now and forever dwell Thou in me;
Thou, my Protector, Shield and Defender,
Draw me and keep me closer to Thee.

FANNY CROSBY

We too, O our Redeemer, prostrate ourselves before your Cross in the transports of our love, and we will repeat before the whole world the song that the angels chant ceaselessly in heaven: "The lamb that was sacrificed is worthy to receive power and divinity and might and wisdom and honor and glory and blessing." Amen.

FATHER FORTIN

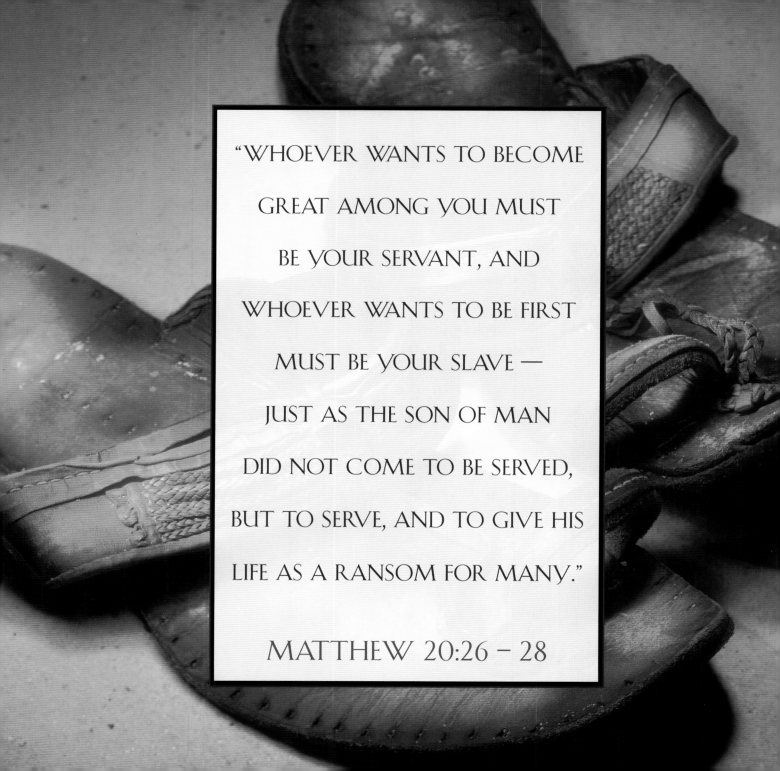

"WHOEVER WANTS TO BECOME

GREAT AMONG YOU MUST

BE YOUR SERVANT, AND

WHOEVER WANTS TO BE FIRST

MUST BE YOUR SLAVE —

JUST AS THE SON OF MAN

DID NOT COME TO BE SERVED,

BUT TO SERVE, AND TO GIVE HIS

LIFE AS A RANSOM FOR MANY."

MATTHEW 20:26 – 28

JESUS

SON *of* MAN

When I look at Jesus' warm and intimate friendships, my heart fills with praise that Jesus was . . . a man. A man of flesh-and-blood reality. His heart felt the sting of sympathy. His eyes glowed with tenderness. His arms embraced. His lips smiled. His hands touched. Jesus was male! Jesus invites us to relate to him as the Son of Man. And because he is fully man, we can relate to Jesus with affection and love.

JONI EARECKSON TADA

On the Mount of Ascension the transfiguration was completed, and our Lord went back to his primal glory; but he did not go back simply as Son of God: He went back as Son of Man as well as Son of God. That means there is freedom of access now for anyone straight to the very throne of God through the ascension of the Son of Man. At his ascension our Lord entered heaven, and he keeps the door open for humanity to enter.

OSWALD CHAMBERS

With Jesus' incarnation, Eternity steps into Time, and Time loses itself in Eternity. Hence Jesus; in the eyes of God, a man, and in the eyes of men, God. It is sublimely simple; a transcendental soap opera going on century after century and touching innumerable hearts; from some bleak, lonely soul seeking a hand to hold when all others have been withdrawn, to vast concourses of joyful believers singing their glorias.

MALCOLM MUGGERIDGE

'Tis God's own Image and withal,

The Son of Man, that mortals all

May find in Him a Brother.

He comes, with peace and love to bide

On earth, the erring race to guide

And help as could no other;

Rather gather closer, fonder,

Sheep that wander, feed and fold
    them,

Than let evil powers hold them.

JOHAN OLOF WALLIN

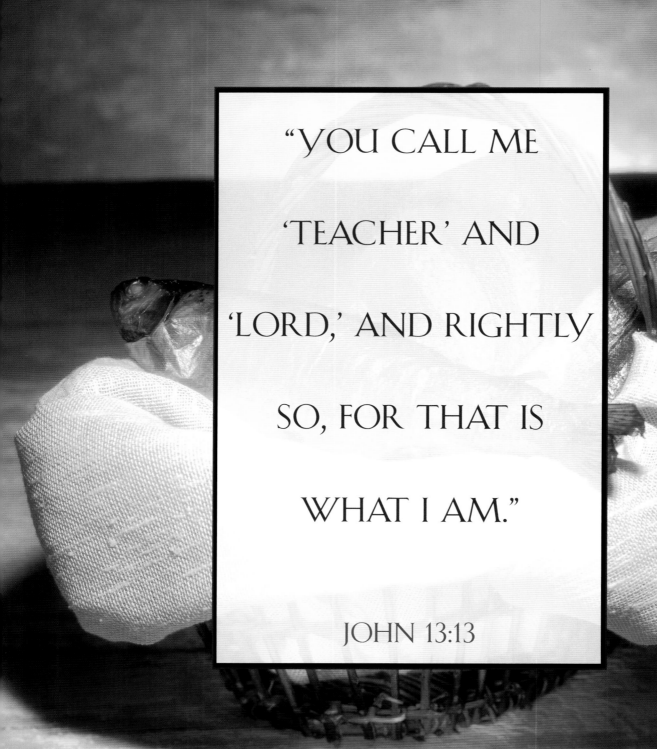

"YOU CALL ME
'TEACHER' AND
'LORD,' AND RIGHTLY
SO, FOR THAT IS
WHAT I AM."

JOHN 13:13

JESUS

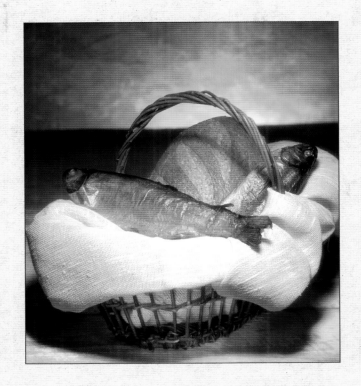

TEACHER

If I had sought a one-word
label to describe Jesus to his con-
temporaries, I would have chosen
the word rabbi, or teacher. By any
account, Jesus was a master
teacher. Followers were drawn by
the magnetic power of his words.
Jesus' answers cut to the heart of
the question and to the hearts of
his listeners. I doubt I would have
left any encounter with Jesus feel-
ing smug or self-satisfied.

PHILIP YANCEY

A man who was merely a man and said the sort of things Jesus said would not be a great moral teacher. He would either be a lunatic—on the level with the man who says he is a poached egg—or else he would be the Devil of Hell. Either this man was, and is, the Son of God; or else a madman or something worse.

C. S. LEWIS

Christ was a true Teacher. He taught the truth. He was able to make Himself understood to men of low estate. He used words which men could comprehend. He illustrated His messages in a practical manner. "The common people heard Him gladly." That was a high compliment indeed.

T. C. HORTON &
CHARLES E. HURLBURT

O teach me, Lord, that I may teach
The precious things Thou dost impart;
And wing my words, that they may reach
The hidden depths of many a heart.

FRANCES RIDLEY HAVERGAL

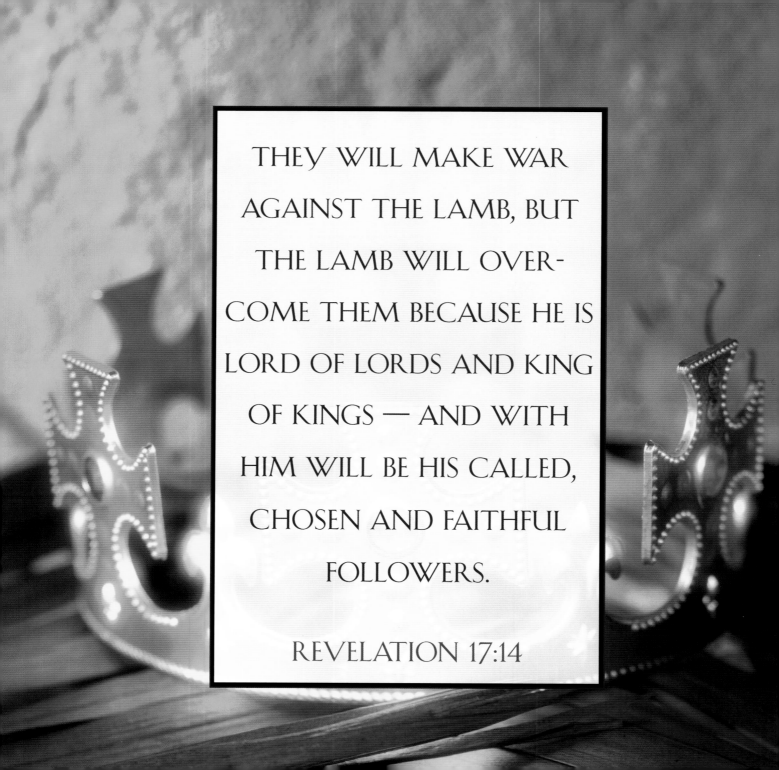

THEY WILL MAKE WAR AGAINST THE LAMB, BUT THE LAMB WILL OVERCOME THEM BECAUSE HE IS LORD OF LORDS AND KING OF KINGS — AND WITH HIM WILL BE HIS CALLED, CHOSEN AND FAITHFUL FOLLOWERS.

REVELATION 17:14

JESUS

KING of KINGS

Our God has established the Kingdom of heaven—or Kingdom of God—His Kingdom. He invites us to become citizens of that community. He extends an invitation to us to become Christians (Christ's men and women). He welcomes us to give our allegiance to Christ, the King of kings.

W. PHILLIP KELLER

Who is the King of kings? The One who was born in a manger and who fellowshiped with fishermen as he longs to fellowship with us today. A sharp sword issues from his mouth—the sword of the Spirit, which is the Word of God. As his enemies fell before his presence in the Garden, so they will always fall. The power of God's Word is irresistible. How foolish are they whose feeble hands are raised up against the King of Kings—the Mighty One.

**T. C. HORTON &
CHARLES E. HURLBURT**

The head that once was crowned
with thorns
Is crowned with glory now;
A royal diadem adorns
The mighty victor's brow.

The highest place that heaven affords
Belongs to Him by right;
The King of kings and Lord of lords,
And heaven's eternal light.

THOMAS KELLY

Crown of thorns and staff of spite,
Must you mock our Sovereign's
    might?
Know you not whom Pilate brings?
Jesus Christ, the King of kings!

Road of sorrow, lead the way
To redeeming love today.
Let me see my Savior's face;
Let me taste this gift of grace.

ROBERT CULLINAN

SELECTIONS TAKEN FROM:

A Way of Seeing, (Grand Rapids: Fleming H. Revell, 1977).

Names of Christ, (Chicago: Moody Bible Institute, 1994).

One Quiet Moment, (Eugene, Ore: Harvest House Publishers, 1997).

Following Christ, (Grand Rapids, Mich.: Zondervan Publishing House, 1996).

Diamonds in the Dust, (Grand Rapids, Mich.: Zondervan Publishing House, 1993).

The Wonderful Names of Our Wonderful Lord, (Plainfield, New Jersey: Logos International).

The Names of Jesus, (Grand Rapids, Mich.: Baker Books, 1997).

The Christian's Secret of a Happy Life, (Barbour and Company, 1985).

RAGMAN: And Other Cries of Faith, (San Francisco: HarperSanFrancisco, Zondervan Publishing House, 1984).

Walking With God, (Grand Rapids, Mich.: Fleming H. Revell, 1980).

"O Lord Jesus, Lamb of God," Copyright 1996, Robert Cullinan. The copyright holder grants permission to reproduce these lyrics, as long as this notice remains with each copy.

Growing Deep in the Christian Life, (Sisters, Ore.: Multnomah Press).

Pulpit Legends: *Two Hundred and Eight Titles and Symbols of Christ*, (Chattanooga, Tenn.: AMG Publishers, 1994).

Out of the Saltshaker, (Carol Stream, Ill: InterVarsity Press, 1979).

100 Meditations for Advent and Christmas, (Nashville, Tenn.: The Upper Room, 1994).

The Jesus I Never Knew, (Grand Rapids, Mich.: Zondervan Publishing House, 1995).

The Gospel According to Jesus, (Grand Rapids, Mich.: Zondervan Publishing House, 1994).

My Utmost for His Highest, (Grand Rapids, Mich.: Discovery House Publishers, 1935 by Mead & Dodd).

Parish Sermons, 1855.

The Heidelberg Catechism.

When God Weeps, (Grand Rapids, Mich.: Zondervan Publishing House, 1997).

The Love of God, (Grand Rapids, Mich.: Discovery House Publishers, 1985).

Jesus: *The Man Who Lives*, (New York: HarperCollins, 1975).

C.S. Lewis, *Mere Christianity*, (The Macmillan Company).